AF725726

Dedicated to all those that struggle

then achieve.

To:My daughter Josie and my grandson Francis

Myler's
Autism & Aspergers Syndrome

A New Perspective

Copyright © 2025

No part of this publication may be reproduced, stored in a retrieval system, or transmitted in any form or by any means, electronic, mechanical, photocopying, recording, or otherwise, without the prior written permission of the publisher.

First Edition: 2025

This copyright page includes the necessary copyright notice, permissions request information, acknowledgments for the cover design, interior design, and editing, as well as the details of the first edition.

Disclaimer: This book is a work of non-fiction and is intended solely for informational and educational purposes. The names mentioned within are trademarks of their respective owners. This publication is not affiliated with, endorsed by, or sponsored by any of these trademark holders. The inclusion of these names is meant to provide context and historical reference.

The author does not claim ownership of any trademarks or copyrights related to the names and likenesses of the individuals referenced in this book. Any opinions expressed herein are those of the author and do not necessarily reflect the views of any organization or trademark holder.

Support Local Groby Authors

Books By Dr Stephen F Myler PhD

Psychological Warfare

Criminology

Travel Biog

Fiction

Psychology

Http://book.by/stephen-f-myler.

Also available on Amazon Kindle UK

Introduction

Imagine stepping into a world where the usual rules of socializing, talking, and perceiving flip upside down—sometimes subtly, sometimes like a lightning strike. It's a world where how the brain processes info creates a whole new lens on life—one that uncovers hidden talents, fierce passions, and perspectives that challenge everything you thought you knew about human connection. Welcome to the realm of autism and Asperger's, a landscape packed with complexity, strength, and untapped potential.

For ages, autism's been misunderstood, mostly boxed in as a set of challenges and limitations. But beneath that surface lies a vibrant spectrum—abilities and experiences that don't fit into neat boxes. Folks on the spectrum often navigate sensory worlds that can either overwhelm or inspire. They cling to routines for stability, communicate in ways that sometimes go beyond words, and have passions that run deep. Their memories are sharp, insights priceless. Yet, the social rules most people take for granted? They can feel like a secret code—elusive, frustrating, yet deeply yearned for.

This book isn't just about facts or stereotypes. It's an invitation—to see through fresh eyes, to embrace the full humanity of those on the spectrum. You'll learn how sensory input shapes everyday life, how emotions can hit with seismic force, and how alternative ways of communicating can unlock understanding. You'll meet stories of victory and struggle—people who've harnessed their unique wiring to shine in art, science, and everything in between.

But hey, it's more than just understanding individuals. It's about recognizing the power of support networks, the importance of acceptance, and the hope for a future where neurodiversity isn't just tolerated but celebrated. Around the world, experiences vary, reminding us that inclusion isn't just a local issue; it's a global mission. Early diagnosis, customized education, meaningful jobs—these aren't just checkboxes. They're pathways to unlocking potential, dignity, and respect.

As you flip through these pages, expect to get a peek into how the brain works—how genetics and environment dance together, how cutting-edge research is reshaping possibilities. More than that, you'll see that autism isn't a limitation but a different way of being—a way that adds to the richness of our shared human story.

This isn't just a guide; it's a call to broaden your view, challenge assumptions, and celebrate minds that make our world extraordinary. Whether you're a parent, teacher, professional, or just curious, the stories and insights here will inspire you to see autism and Asperger's in a new light—one full of hope, respect, and endless possibilities. Get ready for a journey that might just change how you think about difference, connection, and what it really means to be human.

Table of Contents

Chapter 1: Understanding Autism and Asperger's Syndrome
How autism and Asperger's affect the brain differently
Why people with Asperger's often have strong focus on specific interests
How social communication challenges vary widely among individuals

Chapter 2: The Sensory World of Autism
Why some sounds, lights, or textures feel overwhelming
How sensory experiences can be both a challenge and a strength
Ways to create comfortable environments for sensory differences

Chapter 3: The Power of Routine and Predictability
Why many with autism prefer routines and what happens when they change
How routines can help reduce anxiety and increase confidence
Creative ways to introduce flexibility without causing stress

Chapter 4: Communication Beyond Words
How body language and facial expressions can be confusing
The role of alternative communication methods like pictures or technology
Why some people with autism prefer written or typed communication

Chapter 5: The Hidden Talents in Autism
Examples of extraordinary memory, math skills, or artistic abilities
How focusing on strengths can improve self-esteem and opportunities
Stories of famous people who may have had autism or Asperger's

Chapter 6: Understanding Social Challenges
Why social rules can feel like a secret code
How misunderstandings can happen even when trying to connect
Ways to teach social skills that feel natural and useful

Chapter 7: Emotions and Autism
How emotions might be felt very strongly or in unexpected ways
Why it can be hard to explain feelings to others
Techniques to recognize and manage emotions effectively

Chapter 8: The Role of Interests and Passions
How deep interests help build knowledge and confidence
Why some people with autism might talk about their favorite topics a lot
Using passions as a bridge to connect with others

Chapter 9: The Importance of Support Networks
How family, friends, and professionals help build success
Why understanding and patience make a big difference

Examples of helpful support strategies in schools and communities

Chapter 10: Autism in Different Cultures
How autism is viewed and treated around the world
Why cultural beliefs affect diagnosis and support
Stories of diverse experiences that broaden understanding

Chapter 11: The Journey of Diagnosis
What happens during an autism assessment
Why early diagnosis can change outcomes
How families and individuals feel during the process

Chapter 12: Autism and Education
How learning styles can be different for students with autism
Why personalized teaching methods improve learning
Examples of successful classroom adaptations

Chapter 13: Employment and Autism
Why many adults with autism want meaningful work
How workplaces can be adjusted for different needs
Success stories of people finding jobs that fit their skills

Chapter 14: The Future of Autism Research
New technologies helping understand the brain
How genetics and environment might influence autism
Exciting possibilities for better support and treatments

Chapter 15: Celebrating Neurodiversity

Why being different is valuable and important
How society benefits from diverse ways of thinking
Ways to promote acceptance and inclusion everywhere

Chapter 16: Notes on Austism Diagnosis and Treatment.

YOU DON'T LOOK AUTISTIC.

YOU DON'T SEEM ADHD.

YOU DON'T COME ACROSS AS NEURODIVERGENT

BUT

NEURODIVERGENCE DOESN'T HAVE A 'LOOK'.

LISTEN. UNDERSTAND. INCLUDE.

Chapter 1

Understanding Autism and Asperger's Syndrome

Autism and Asperger's syndrome are terms you often hear together, but they're not exactly the same. Both are part of what's called autism spectrum disorder, or ASD, which is a way to describe a range of brain differences that affect how people think, feel, and interact. Even though they share some features, the way the brain works in each case can be quite different. To really understand these differences, it helps to look at how the brain's wiring influences behavior, interests, and social skills.

Let's start with autism in general. When scientists look at brains of people with autism, they find that the connections between different parts of the brain don't always work the same way as in most people. Think of the brain as a network of roads that carry information. In autism, some roads might be too busy, too quiet, or not connected properly. This can make it harder for the brain to process sensory information, like sounds or lights, or to understand social cues, like facial expressions or tone of voice. It can also lead to repetitive behaviors or intense focus on certain interests.

For example, someone with autism might find loud noises overwhelming because their brain processes sensory input differently. They might also have trouble figuring out what someone's feelings are just by looking at their face, because the part of the brain that helps with social understanding isn't working the same way. The overall pattern is that the brain's different parts don't always communicate smoothly, which makes it hard to put together the big picture of social situations or sensory experiences.

Now, let's talk about Asperger's syndrome. For a long time, it was considered a separate diagnosis, but today it's generally grouped under autism spectrum disorder. People with Asperger's usually have average or above-average intelligence and don't have significant delays in language development — meaning they start talking at the usual age and can speak fluently. But their brains have some differences, especially in areas linked to planning, attention, and controlling impulses. This can explain why many with Asperger's are very focused on certain topics or activities.

One of the most noticeable features of Asperger's is what's called "special interests." These are intense, often detailed passions about specific subjects like trains, computers, or history. Unlike hobbies most people have, these interests can take up a lot of time and energy. When someone with Asperger's is engaged in their favorite topic, they often feel very rewarded and motivated. This is because their brain's reward system releases dopamine — a chemical that makes us feel good — when they focus on something they love. This creates a loop: the more they focus on their interest, the more they want to learn about it, and the more rewarding it feels.

This focus isn't just a hobby; it's a core part of how their brain works. People with Asperger's tend to notice details that others might overlook. For example, they might be able to remember facts about a topic in incredible depth or pick up on small changes in a pattern. This detail-oriented way of thinking can lead to expertise in areas like math, music, technology, or history. But it can also make it hard to switch attention to other things or to see the bigger picture. Their brains prioritize depth over breadth, which shapes how they learn and how they see the world.

Social skills are another big area where autism and Asperger's differ. Social communication isn't the same for everyone on the spectrum. Some might struggle a lot with understanding nonverbal cues like facial expressions, gestures, or tone of voice. Others might find it hard to start conversations or keep them going. Some may take things very literally, missing sarcasm or jokes. These differences come from how their brains process social information, especially in regions like the amygdala and the superior temporal sulcus, which are involved in understanding others.

But here's an important point: social difficulties aren't just about being shy or awkward. They reflect a different way of perceiving and engaging with the world. For example, someone with Asperger's might be very honest and direct because they process social rules differently. They might not see the point in small talk or might prefer straightforward conversations. Their brains focus more on logical consistency rather than emotional nuance. Sometimes, this can lead to misunderstandings, but it also means they bring unique perspectives to conversations.

It's also worth noting that the level of social challenge varies widely. Some people with Asperger's develop strong social skills and can navigate many situations on their own. Others might need support to understand social norms or to build relationships. This variation depends on many factors, including early support, education, and family environment. The brain's plasticity — its ability to change and adapt — means that with help, many can improve their social skills over time.

Understanding these differences is key to fostering empathy. When we see autism and Asperger's as variations in how the brain works, it becomes easier to see the strengths and challenges each person has. It's not just about deficits but about different ways of thinking and feeling. Recognizing this helps us move away from stereotypes and toward more tailored support — whether in school, work, or social settings.

So, what does all this mean? Basically, autism and Asperger's show us how diverse human brains can be. Differences in how brains connect and process information shape how people focus, communicate, and relate to others. The intense interests seen in Asperger's come from how their reward system works and their attention to detail. Meanwhile, social challenges are rooted in how certain brain regions handle social cues and emotional understanding.

By understanding these neurological and behavioral nuances, we can be more compassionate. We can see that everyone's brain is a little different, and that's okay. Some people might need more support with social skills, while others excel in areas like memory or pattern recognition. The goal isn't to "fix" people but to appreciate their unique ways of seeing the world and to help them thrive.

In the end, recognizing the diversity within autism and Asperger's isn't just about science. It's about respecting different minds and creating a society where everyone feels understood and valued. When we look beyond labels and focus on individual strengths and needs, we open the door to more inclusive communities and richer human connections.

Chapter 2

The Sensory World of Autism

When you think about the world, what comes to mind? The sounds, the sights, the feel of things around you? For many folks, it's just a regular day. But for individuals with autism, that same world can feel like a wild, chaotic storm. It's not just noise; it's a *cacophony*. Lights are brighter, sounds are sharper, and textures can be downright maddening. Picture this: you're in a café, and the chatter of voices feels like a thousand horns blaring. That's the reality for many with autism. Everyday life can turn into a sensory minefield.

Sensory Sensitivity: A Double-Edged Sword

So, what's going on here? A lot of people on the spectrum have heightened sensitivity to sensory input. That means what might be a mild distraction for you could feel like a full-blown assault for them. Imagine the hum of a refrigerator—just a background noise for most, but for someone with autism, it could be like a jet engine roaring in their ears. And those bright lights? They can feel like lasers cutting through the darkness.

Let's not sugarcoat it: this overload can lead to some serious anxiety. Meltdowns? Yep, they happen. Withdrawal from social situations? Absolutely. It's crucial to understand why these reactions occur. The brain of someone with autism processes sensory information differently. Research shows that differences in neural connectivity and sensory pathways can make it tough for their brains to filter out the irrelevant noise. It's like walking into a packed room where every single sound, sight, and smell is fighting for your attention. For them, that's amplified to a level that's hard to comprehend.

Turning Sensory Challenges into Strengths

But here's the kicker: sensory experiences aren't just a source of discomfort. They can also be strengths! Many individuals with autism possess a keen awareness of their surroundings. Some can pick up on subtle sounds that would fly right over most people's heads. Others might notice intricate visual details that others miss. This heightened perception can lead to some pretty amazing skills—think music, art, or even memory. By recognizing and nurturing these strengths, caregivers and educators can help individuals with autism channel their sensory experiences into something positive.

Creating Comfortable Spaces

So, how do we help? First off, creating environments that are comfy and supportive is key. Simple tweaks can make a world of difference. Dim lights? Yes, please! Soft, muted colors? Sign me up! These adjustments can help tone down visual overload. And if sounds are an issue, noise-canceling headphones or earplugs can be lifesavers. They allow individuals to engage in social settings without feeling like they're drowning in a sea of noise.

Let's not forget about textures. Some people are super

sensitive to certain fabrics or surfaces, while others crave tactile experiences. Offering a range of textures—like cozy blankets, squishy toys, or even textured wall panels—can provide positive sensory engagement. It's all about paying attention to individual preferences. If a kid finds comfort in fidget toys, make sure they've got access to them during stressful moments.

The Power of Routine

Another biggie? Routines. Many individuals with autism thrive on predictability. It gives them a sense of control in a world that can feel chaotic. Visual schedules can be a game-changer. They help individuals anticipate changes in their environment, reducing the anxiety that can come from unexpected sensory experiences. Clear expectations for transitions can make adapting to new situations way easier.

Navigating Social Interactions

Now, let's chat about social interactions. They can be a minefield, especially in sensory-rich environments. Understanding the social dynamics can help create more inclusive spaces. Think about it: smaller gatherings in quieter settings can lead to better communication and less sensory overload. And encouraging open conversations about sensory preferences? That's a win! It empowers individuals to speak up for their needs, giving them a sense of agency in their interactions.

The Role of Educators

In schools, teachers play a massive role in accommodating

sensory differences. Crafting sensory-friendly classrooms can enhance learning experiences for students with autism. This might mean setting up quiet zones, using visual aids to boost communication, and incorporating sensory breaks into the daily grind. When educators prioritize sensory needs, they create an environment where every student feels valued and supported.

Empathy and Awareness: The Key Ingredients

Ultimately, understanding the sensory world of autism is all about empathy and awareness. Recognizing that sensory experiences can be both challenging and empowering allows us to create environments that foster growth. Embracing sensory differences means letting individuals with autism shine, unlocking their potential and celebrating their unique perspectives. Through thoughtful accommodations and supportive strategies, we can help them navigate their sensory landscapes with confidence.

A Journey of Discovery

So, where does that leave us? The sensory world of autism is complex and multifaceted. By acknowledging the overwhelming nature of certain stimuli and recognizing the strengths that come from heightened sensory awareness, we can support individuals with autism in meaningful ways. As we strive to understand and accommodate sensory differences, we pave the way for a more inclusive society that values neurodiversity and promotes acceptance.

Celebrating Richness in Human Experience

This journey toward understanding autism’s sensory world isn’t just about tackling challenges; it’s also about celebrating the richness of human experience. We’re all different, and that’s what makes life interesting. When we embrace those differences, we create a world that’s not only more inclusive but also more vibrant.

Imagine a society where everyone feels valued, where sensory differences are seen as strengths rather than weaknesses. That’s the goal, right? We can make it happen through empathy, understanding, and a willingness to adapt. The sensory landscape of autism may be overwhelming at times, but it’s also filled with potential.

Let’s Make a Change

So, let’s take action. Let’s create environments that support and uplift individuals with autism. Whether it’s in our homes, schools, or communities, small changes can lead to big impacts. Let’s listen to their needs, advocate for their rights, and celebrate their unique contributions.

At the end of the day, it’s all about connection. By fostering understanding and acceptance, we can build bridges that connect us all, regardless of our sensory experiences. So, let’s get to work! Together, we can make the world a more inclusive, accepting place for everyone.

The Bottom Line

The sensory world of autism is a rich tapestry woven with both challenges and strengths. By acknowledging the complexities of sensory experiences and creating supportive environments, we can help individuals with autism thrive. It's not just about accommodating differences; it's about celebrating them. As we embark on this journey together, let's remember that every person has something unique to offer. Embrace those differences, and let's create a world where everyone feels at home.

Chapter 3

The Power of Routine and Predictability

Routines are like the glue that holds daily life together for folks with autism. It's not just a quirky preference; it's about how their brains work. You see, many people on the spectrum thrive in structured environments and predictable schedules. For them, routines create a bubble of safety in a world that often feels chaotic. When they know what's coming next, they can focus on engaging with life instead of worrying about what might happen.

Why is routine so crucial? It goes back to the unique wiring of an autistic brain. These brains often seek patterns and familiarity, which can show up in various ways. Some might stick to a strict daily schedule, while others have specific activities they prefer to repeat. If something disrupts these patterns—like a change in the timing of a favorite activity or an unexpected visitor—it can throw them for a loop. This isn't just about liking things a certain way; it's a deeply rooted response to threats against their stability.

When routines get shaken up, anxiety can bubble over, leading to meltdowns or shutdowns. These reactions aren't just tantrums; they're genuine struggles to cope with overwhelming sensory and emotional inputs. Imagine your whole world flipping upside down just because someone changed the plan. That's how it feels for many autistic individuals. So, establishing routines isn't just about comfort; it's also about emotional balance.

Routines can also boost confidence. When autistic individuals engage in familiar activities, they're more likely to succeed. And success? Well, it breeds confidence. Take a kid who knows Saturday mornings mean a trip to the library. They can look forward to picking out books, chatting with librarians, or joining reading programs. That predictability helps them shine, building their self-esteem and encouraging them to branch out and try new things.

But here's the kicker: life's unpredictable. While routines are great, it's important to weave in some flexibility. How do you do that without causing a meltdown? Creative strategies can help ease transitions from rigid routines to more adaptable ones. One solid approach is prepping individuals for changes ahead of time. If you know a routine is going to shift, consider using a visual schedule that lays out what's changing. A simple chart can show the day's activities, highlighting what's different and what stays the same.

Visual aids can be a game-changer. Using symbols or pictures to represent activities can make the idea of change less daunting. This way, individuals can see the new routine next to the familiar stuff, which helps calm those anxious feelings. Plus, getting them involved in planning can empower them. If there's a family outing, for example, discussing the itinerary and letting them pick activities gives them a sense of control.

Another effective tactic is to introduce changes gradually. Instead of a sudden overhaul, think small adjustments over time. If a child has a strict bedtime routine, consider mixing it up a bit—maybe read a different book or change the order of activities. This slow approach lets them adjust without feeling overwhelmed.

And let's not forget about teaching coping strategies. Equipping individuals with tools to handle unexpected changes is vital. Mindfulness techniques—like deep breathing or grounding exercises—can help manage anxiety when routines go haywire. Encouraging open conversations about feelings can also provide an outlet for discomfort. When talking about emotions becomes normal, navigating change feels a bit less scary.

Now, incorporating flexibility doesn't mean ditching structure altogether. It's about striking a balance between predictability and adaptability. By highlighting the importance of routine while also teaching the skills to handle change, individuals with autism can build resilience. They can learn that while routines offer comfort, change is a part of life that can be tackled head-on.

At the end of the day, we want to create an environment where individuals feel secure yet empowered to explore. Routines can lay the groundwork for growth, helping autistic individuals build confidence and skills that'll serve them well into adulthood. With the right strategies, they can learn to embrace both the familiar and the unknown, allowing them to thrive in an ever-changing world.

So, let's wrap this up. Understanding the power of routine and predictability in the lives of individuals with autism is crucial. Recognizing why these structures matter can lead to more compassionate and effective support strategies. By easing anxiety and building confidence through routines, we can help individuals navigate their world more smoothly. Plus, by introducing flexibility thoughtfully, we can prepare them for life's unpredictability while keeping the comfort of routines intact. This balance? It's not just beneficial; it's essential for promoting a sense of agency and well-being in individuals with autism.

The Importance of Routines

Routines aren't just a preference; they're often a necessity. For many individuals with autism, the world can feel like a whirlwind. Routines provide a sense of order, a familiar rhythm to their day. Imagine waking up every morning knowing exactly what to expect. Breakfast at the same time, a specific route to school, and the same schedule in class. That predictability can be incredibly calming.

Now, think about it—what happens when that routine gets disrupted? Maybe the bus is late, or a teacher decides to switch up the lesson plan. Suddenly, that comforting structure is gone, and anxiety kicks in. It's like being tossed into a storm without a life jacket. For many, this anxiety isn't just a fleeting feeling; it can lead to significant distress, manifesting as meltdowns or shutdowns.

It's crucial to understand that these reactions are not just overreactions. They stem from a genuine struggle to cope with the unpredictability of life. When routines are disrupted, it can feel like the ground is shifting beneath their feet. This is why creating and maintaining routines is essential—not just for comfort, but for emotional regulation.

Building Confidence Through Familiarity

Let's dive deeper into how routines can boost confidence. When individuals with autism engage in familiar activities, they're more likely to succeed. And success? That's a big deal. It's like planting seeds of confidence that can grow into a garden of exploration. Picture a child who knows every Saturday means a trip to the local park. They get to play their favorite games, interact with other kids, and even help pack the picnic. That predictability not only makes them feel good; it also gives them the confidence to try new things.

Confidence is a powerful motivator. When someone feels competent in one area, they're more likely to take risks in others. Maybe that child who loves the park will decide to join a sports team or try a new hobby. Routines can act as a launchpad for exploration, giving individuals the courage to step outside their comfort zones.

The Balancing Act: Flexibility vs. Structure

Now, here's where it gets tricky. While routines are fantastic, life is full of surprises. That's why finding a balance between structure and flexibility is key. It's not about throwing routines out the window; it's about adapting them. So how do you introduce flexibility without sending someone into a tailspin?

One effective strategy is to prepare individuals for upcoming changes. If you know a routine is going to shift, give them a heads-up. Use visual schedules or social stories to outline what's going to happen. This way, they can mentally prepare for the change instead of being blindsided by it.

Involving individuals in the planning process can also make a huge difference. Let's say there's a family outing. Discuss the itinerary together, and let them choose activities. This not only gives them a sense of control but also makes them feel valued. It's a win-win!

Gradual Changes: A Gentle Approach

Another approach is to make changes gradually. Instead of a sudden switch, think about small tweaks that can be integrated over time. If a child has a strict bedtime routine, consider introducing minor variations—like reading a different book or swapping out activities. This slow approach helps them adjust without feeling overwhelmed.

And let's not forget about teaching coping strategies. Equipping individuals with tools to handle unexpected changes is vital. Mindfulness techniques—like deep breathing or grounding exercises—can help manage anxiety when routines go haywire. Encouraging open conversations about feelings can also provide an outlet for discomfort. When talking about emotions becomes normal, navigating change feels a bit less scary.

Resilience Through Routine

Ultimately, the goal is to create an environment where individuals feel secure yet empowered to explore. Routines can serve as a foundation for growth, helping individuals with autism build confidence and skills that will serve them throughout their lives. With the right strategies in place, they can learn to embrace both the familiar and the unknown, allowing them to thrive in an ever-changing world.

Conclusion: A Call for Understanding

So, let's wrap this up. Understanding the power of routine and predictability in the lives of individuals with autism is crucial. Recognizing why these structures matter can lead to more compassionate and effective support strategies. By easing anxiety and building confidence through routines, we can help individuals navigate their world more smoothly. Plus, by introducing flexibility thoughtfully, we can prepare them for life's unpredictability while keeping the comfort of routines intact. This balance? It's not just beneficial; it's essential for promoting a sense of agency and well-being in individuals with autism.

In the end, it's all about creating a space where individuals can feel secure while also having the freedom to explore and grow. Routines provide that structure, but flexibility allows for growth. Together, they create a harmonious environment where individuals with autism can thrive.

Chapter 4

Communication Beyond Words: A Journey into Understanding

Navigating the communication landscape can be a real maze, especially for folks with autism and Asperger's Syndrome. For many, those subtle cues—like body language and facial expressions—can feel like a foreign language. Misunderstandings pop up, leading to frustration and confusion. In social settings, these non-verbal signals are like the unsung heroes of conversation. But for those on the autism spectrum, figuring out these signals can feel like trying to crack a complex code without all the pieces.

The Puzzle of Body Language

Let's talk about body language. It's a whole mix of gestures, postures, and movements that pack a punch when it comes to meaning. Think about it: a slight shift in stance or a head tilt can say "yes" or "no." A furrowed brow? That might mean someone's confused or worried. For neurotypical folks, these cues come naturally, learned through years of observation and social interaction. But for many on the spectrum, it's like trying to read a book in a language they don't understand.

Take a smile, for instance. Is it genuine? Is it hiding something? That ambiguity can throw a wrench in the works, making effective communication feel like a distant dream. It's like standing in front of a beautiful painting but only seeing the frame—missing out on the masterpiece inside.

Facial Expressions: The Double-Edged Sword

Now, let's dive into facial expressions. A frown usually screams sadness, right? But for someone with autism, that same frown might be read as anger or disapproval. Talk about a recipe for social anxiety! Imagine second-guessing every interaction, feeling like you're walking on eggshells. The fear of making a social blunder can push people away, robbing them of the chance to connect and make friends.

Bridging the Gap: Alternative Communication Methods

But hey, there's good news! Alternative communication methods have popped up as lifesavers for many. Visual supports, like pictures and symbols, can help clear the fog. Take Picture Exchange Communication Systems (PECS), for example. This nifty tool lets individuals communicate their needs by swapping images. It's a game-changer, reducing frustration and giving folks a sense of independence. Imagine being able to express yourself in a way that feels right for you—that's powerful!

And let's not forget about technology. Apps designed for individuals with autism are stepping up to the plate, offering everything from text-to-speech features to customizable visual aids. These tools make it easier to share thoughts without the pressure of decoding non-verbal cues on the fly. Technology isn't just about enhancing communication; it's about giving people a voice—a way to advocate for themselves and express their feelings clearly.

The Power of the Written Word

A lot of folks with autism lean toward written or typed communication. Why? Because it gives them control and clarity that can be missing in spoken exchanges. When spoken language feels overwhelming, writing becomes a safe haven. It allows for organizing thoughts and expressing ideas without the pressure of a ticking clock in face-to-face conversations.

And guess what? This preference often extends to social media and online platforms. The beauty of the digital world is that it lets people engage at their own pace. No rush, no anxiety. Just pure, unfiltered expression. Online spaces can be a goldmine for connection, where interests can be shared and friendships can blossom without the usual communication hurdles.

Every Individual is Unique

Now, here's the kicker: every individual is different. Communication preferences can vary like the colors in a rainbow. Some might thrive in face-to-face chats with the right support, while others might find peace in written communication. It's all about understanding these preferences. Family, educators, and friends play a huge role in creating an inclusive environment that respects diverse communication styles.

Building Bridges with Awareness and Patience

To really support individuals with autism in their communication journey, we gotta cultivate awareness and patience. Taking the time to understand how someone prefers to communicate can make a world of difference. Active listening is key—paying attention not just to the words but to how they're expressed. When people feel heard and understood, they're way more likely to open up and engage.

Teaching social skills that incorporate alternative communication methods can also be a game-changer. Role-playing scenarios that use visual aids or written communication can be super helpful. It's like giving individuals a toolbox filled with strategies to tackle social situations with confidence. These exercises can take the mystery out of social interactions, equipping individuals with the skills they need to express themselves effectively.

A Rich Tapestry of Experiences

In the end, communication beyond words is a rich tapestry of experiences for those with autism and Asperger's Syndrome. Sure, body language and facial expressions can throw a wrench in the works, but alternative communication methods—like visual supports and technology—offer pathways to connection. Recognizing the preference for written communication can further enhance understanding and engagement.

By fostering an environment of awareness, patience, and support, we can create spaces where individuals feel empowered to communicate authentically. It's all about paving the way for deeper connections and meaningful relationships.

Personal Anecdote: A Journey of Understanding

Let me share a little story. A friend of mine has a son on the autism spectrum. At first, conversations felt like a constant game of charades. We'd sit at the dinner table, and I'd throw out questions, but he'd just stare at his plate. It was tough. But then, we tried using pictures to communicate. Suddenly, the walls started coming down. He'd pick out images of his favorite foods or activities, and it was like a light bulb went off. We found a way to connect, and it was beautiful.

The Role of Community

Community support is another piece of the puzzle. When family and friends come together to understand and accommodate different communication styles, it creates a safety net. Imagine a community where everyone's on the same page, working together to foster inclusion. That's the kind of world we should strive for.

Encouraging Self-Advocacy

And let's not forget about self-advocacy. Encouraging individuals to speak up about their preferences can be empowering. It's like handing them the microphone and saying, "Your voice matters!" Whether it's through visual aids, written communication, or technology, giving them the tools to express themselves is crucial.

The Future of Communication

Looking ahead, the future of communication for individuals with autism is bright. As technology advances, so do the tools available for enhancing communication. Imagine virtual reality scenarios that help practice social skills in a safe environment or AI-driven apps that adapt to individual communication styles. The possibilities are endless!

Final Thoughts: Embracing Diversity in Communication

In conclusion, let's embrace the diversity of communication styles. It's not just about finding a common language; it's about celebrating the unique ways individuals express themselves. By fostering understanding, patience, and support, we can create a world where everyone has a voice—where connections are made, friendships flourish, and meaningful relationships thrive.

So, next time you're in a conversation, take a moment to consider the nuances. Communication is more than just words; it's a dance of understanding, a bridge to connection. And in that dance, let's make sure everyone has a chance to lead.

Chapter 5

The Sensory World of Autism

When you think about the world, what pops into your head? The sounds, the sights, the textures? For most folks, it's just another day in the park. But for individuals with autism, that same world can feel like a chaotic whirlwind. It's not merely noise; it's a *cacophony*. Lights are blinding, sounds are piercing, and textures can drive you up the wall. Imagine being in a café where the chatter feels like a thousand horns honking. That's the everyday reality for many people on the spectrum. Life can morph into a sensory battleground.

Sensory Sensitivity: A Double-Edged Sword

So, what's the deal? A lot of people on the autism spectrum experience heightened sensitivity to sensory input. What might be a minor annoyance for you could feel like an all-out assault for them. Picture this: the hum of a refrigerator—just background noise for most, but for someone with autism, it's like a jet engine roaring in their ears. And those bright lights? They can feel like lasers slicing through the darkness.

Let's be real: this overload can crank up anxiety levels. Meltdowns? Yep, they happen. Pulling back from social situations? You bet. It's crucial to grasp why these reactions pop up. An autistic brain processes sensory info differently. Research indicates that variations in neural connections and sensory pathways make it tough for them to filter out the irrelevant noise. It's like stepping into a crowded room where every sound, sight, and smell is vying for your attention. For them, that's cranked up to a level that's hard to wrap your head around.

Turning Sensory Challenges into Strengths

But here's the twist: sensory experiences aren't just sources of discomfort. They can also be strengths! Many individuals with autism have a sharp awareness of their surroundings. Some can catch subtle sounds that would fly right over most people's heads. Others might spot intricate visual details that others miss. This heightened perception can lead to some incredible skills—think music, art, or even memory. By recognizing and nurturing these strengths, caregivers and educators can help individuals with autism channel their sensory experiences into something positive.

Creating Comfortable Spaces

So, how do we help? First off, creating comfy and supportive environments is key. Simple tweaks can make a world of difference. Dim lights? Yes, please! Soft, muted colors? Sign me up! These adjustments can help tone down visual overload. And if sounds are an issue, noise-canceling headphones or earplugs can be lifesavers. They let individuals engage in social settings without feeling like they're drowning in a sea of noise.

And let's talk textures. Some folks are super sensitive to certain fabrics or surfaces, while others crave tactile experiences. Offering a variety of textures—like cozy blankets, squishy toys, or even textured wall panels—can provide positive sensory engagement. It's all about tuning into individual preferences. If a kid finds comfort in fidget toys, make sure they've got access to them during stressful moments.

The Power of Routine

Another biggie? Routines. Many individuals with autism thrive on predictability. It gives them a sense of control in a world that can feel chaotic. Visual schedules can be a game-changer. They help individuals anticipate changes in their environment, reducing the anxiety that can come from unexpected sensory experiences. Clear expectations for transitions can make adapting to new situations way easier.

Navigating Social Interactions

Now, let's chat about social interactions. They can be a minefield, especially in sensory-rich environments. Understanding social dynamics can help create more inclusive spaces. Think about it: smaller gatherings in quieter settings can lead to better communication and less sensory overload. And encouraging open conversations about sensory preferences? That's a win! It empowers individuals to speak up for their needs, giving them a sense of agency in their interactions.

The Role of Educators

In schools, teachers play a massive role in accommodating sensory differences. Crafting sensory-friendly classrooms can enhance learning experiences for students with autism. This might mean setting up quiet zones, using visual aids to boost communication, and incorporating sensory breaks into the daily grind. When educators prioritize sensory needs, they create an environment where every student feels valued and supported.

Empathy and Awareness: The Key Ingredients

Ultimately, understanding the sensory world of autism is all about empathy and awareness. Recognizing that sensory experiences can be both challenging and empowering allows us to create environments that foster growth. Embracing sensory differences means letting individuals with autism shine, unlocking their potential and celebrating their unique perspectives. Through thoughtful accommodations and supportive strategies, we can help them navigate their sensory landscapes with confidence.

A Journey of Discovery

So, where does that leave us? The sensory world of autism is complex and multifaceted. By acknowledging the overwhelming nature of certain stimuli and recognizing the strengths that come from heightened sensory awareness, we can support individuals with autism in meaningful ways. As we strive to understand and accommodate sensory differences, we pave the way for a more inclusive society that values neurodiversity and promotes acceptance.

Celebrating Richness in Human Experience

This journey toward understanding autism's sensory world

isn't just about tackling challenges; it's also about celebrating the richness of human experience. We're all different, and that's what makes life interesting. When we embrace those differences, we create a world that's not only more inclusive but also more vibrant.

Imagine a society where everyone feels valued, where sensory differences are seen as strengths rather than weaknesses. That's the goal, right? We can make it happen through empathy, understanding, and a willingness to adapt. The sensory landscape of autism may be overwhelming at times, but it's also filled with potential.

Let's Make a Change

So, let's take action. Let's create environments that support and uplift individuals with autism. Whether it's in our homes, schools, or communities, small changes can lead to big impacts. Let's listen to their needs, advocate for their rights, and celebrate their unique contributions.

At the end of the day, it's all about connection. By fostering understanding and acceptance, we can build bridges that connect us all, regardless of our sensory experiences. So, let's get to work! Together, we can make the world a more inclusive, accepting place for everyone.

The Bottom Line

The sensory world of autism is a rich tapestry woven with both challenges and strengths. By acknowledging the complexities of sensory experiences and creating supportive environments, we can help individuals with autism thrive. It's not just about accommodating differences; it's about celebrating them. As we embark on this journey together, let's remember that every person has something unique to offer. Embrace those differences, and let's create a world where everyone feels at home.

Understanding the Sensory Overload

Now, let's dig a little deeper into sensory overload. For many on the spectrum, everyday sounds—like a dog barking or the hum of traffic—can feel like a barrage of noise. Imagine standing in front of a speaker at a concert when you're just trying to enjoy the music. That's how it can feel for someone with autism. It's not just annoying; it's overwhelming.

And it doesn't stop at sound. The world is a sensory buffet, and for some, it's too much. Smells that you barely notice can be like a punch in the gut. The smell of food, cologne, or even cleaning products can trigger intense reactions. It's like a rollercoaster ride of sensations that can make everyday life a struggle.

Finding the Right Balance

So, how do we strike a balance? It's all about tuning into the individual. Everyone's sensory preferences are different. What works for one person might not work for another. Some might thrive in a bustling environment, while others need calm and quiet. It's essential to pay attention and adjust accordingly.

And let's not forget about the importance of breaks. Taking time out from overwhelming situations can be a game-changer. Whether it's a quiet corner in a room or a walk outside, giving someone a chance to recharge can help them cope better with sensory input.

The Importance of Communication

Communication is key. It's vital to have open conversations about sensory needs. Ask questions, listen actively, and be receptive to feedback. Encourage individuals to express what they're feeling. Sometimes, they might not have the words, and that's okay. Non-verbal cues can speak volumes. A simple gesture or facial expression can tell you a lot about how someone is feeling.

And hey, let's not forget about technology! There are tons of apps and devices designed to help individuals manage sensory overload. From calming sounds to visual schedules, tech can be a powerful ally in navigating the sensory landscape.

The Role of Community

Communities play a massive role in supporting individuals with autism. It's not just about families and schools; it's about creating an environment where everyone feels included. Local events, support groups, and awareness campaigns can help raise understanding and acceptance. When communities come together, they can create spaces that cater to sensory needs.

Think about it: a community park with quiet zones, sensory-friendly events, and inclusive activities can make a huge difference. It's about creating a culture of acceptance and understanding.

Real-Life Examples of Success

There are countless stories of individuals with autism turning their sensory challenges into strengths. Take the artist who uses their keen eye for detail to create stunning works of art. Or the musician who can hear the tiniest nuances in sound, crafting beautiful melodies. These examples show that sensory experiences can lead to incredible talents.

And let's not forget the everyday heroes—parents, teachers, and friends who advocate for those on the spectrum. Their efforts can change lives. By creating supportive environments and understanding sensory needs, they help individuals thrive.

The Future of Inclusion

Looking ahead, the future of inclusion is bright. As awareness grows, so does the push for better accommodations and understanding. We're starting to see more sensory-friendly spaces in public areas, schools, and workplaces. This shift is crucial for fostering a more inclusive society.

But we can't stop there. It's about continuing the conversation and advocating for change. Whether it's through policy changes or community initiatives, every effort counts. Together, we can create a world where sensory differences are embraced, not just tolerated.

Wrapping It Up

At the end of the day, the sensory world of autism is complex, but it's also filled with potential. By recognizing both the challenges and strengths, we can support individuals in meaningful ways. It's about creating environments that celebrate differences and empower individuals to shine.

So, let's keep pushing for change. Let's build a society where everyone feels valued and understood. Together, we can make a difference, one small step at a time. The journey might be long, but the destination is worth it. Let's make it happen!

Chapter 6

Understanding Social Challenges

Social interactions can often feel like navigating a labyrinth for individuals with autism and Asperger's syndrome. The unwritten rules that govern social behavior can appear as a complex, secret code—one that many people seem to understand intuitively, while others struggle to decipher. This experience can lead to significant misunderstandings, even when the intent to connect is genuine.

Why do these social rules feel like a secret code? For many on the autism spectrum, social cues such as body language, tone of voice, and facial expressions can be perplexing. What may seem like a simple smile to one person might be interpreted differently by someone with autism. This discrepancy can create a barrier to understanding and connecting with others. The subtle nuances of conversation, such as sarcasm or irony, often go unnoticed, leaving individuals feeling lost or frustrated. They may find themselves questioning their interpretations of social situations, leading to anxiety and isolation.

Misunderstandings can arise even when the desire to connect is strong. An individual with autism may approach a conversation with enthusiasm, only to misread a social cue that indicates disinterest from the other person. This can result in awkward silences or abrupt endings to conversations, leaving both parties feeling confused. The individual may leave feeling rejected or misunderstood, while the other person may be unaware of the impact of their nonverbal signals. These interactions can perpetuate a cycle of social anxiety and reluctance to engage, further isolating those who struggle with these challenges.

To address these issues, it is essential to teach social skills in ways that feel natural and useful. Traditional methods of teaching social skills, such as rote memorization or scripted responses, may not resonate with individuals on the spectrum. Instead, a more effective approach involves creating real-life scenarios that allow for practice and exploration. Role-playing can be a valuable tool in this regard, enabling individuals to experience various social situations in a safe environment. This method allows them to experiment with different responses and receive immediate feedback, helping to reinforce learning.

Another effective strategy is to use visual supports, such as social stories or visual schedules. These tools can help clarify social expectations and provide concrete examples of appropriate behaviors in specific contexts. By breaking down complex social interactions into manageable steps, individuals can better understand what is expected of them and how to respond. Additionally, incorporating technology, such as apps designed for social skills training, can engage learners and provide interactive experiences that enhance understanding.

It is also important to foster an environment of empathy and understanding among peers. Teaching neurotypical individuals about autism and the unique challenges faced by their peers can help create a more inclusive atmosphere. By promoting awareness and encouraging patience, we can reduce the stigma surrounding social difficulties and foster meaningful connections.

Ultimately, the goal is to empower individuals with autism to navigate social situations with confidence. By demystifying social rules, addressing misunderstandings, and providing practical tools for skill development, we can help bridge the gap between those on the spectrum and their neurotypical peers. Through understanding and support, we can create a world where everyone feels valued and connected.

Chapter 7

Emotions and Autism: A Deep Dive into the Complex World of Feelings

Navigating the emotional landscape of individuals with autism is no walk in the park. Seriously, it's a bit like trying to solve a Rubik's Cube blindfolded. Emotions can hit hard, often with an intensity that's tough to manage. For those on the spectrum, feelings can be like a rollercoaster—thrilling, yet sometimes downright overwhelming. And let's be real, this can confuse not just the person experiencing it but also their friends and family. The emotional world of someone with autism is often rich and layered, yet it can feel hidden, like a treasure chest buried under layers of sand.

The Intensity of Emotions

First off, let's talk about how people with autism experience emotions. They often feel things more intensely than your average Joe. Think of it this way: while most folks might feel a pleasant buzz of happiness, someone on the spectrum might feel like they've just hit the jackpot. That elation during a favorite activity—like scoring a goal in a soccer game or getting lost in a favorite book—can be exhilarating. But flip the coin, and you might find them grappling with deep sadness or anxiety over a minor change in their routine. It's like having a superpower, but sometimes it feels more like a curse.

Imagine a kid who's just been told they can't play their favorite video game because of a power outage. For a neurotypical kid, it might be a bummer, but for someone with autism, that disappointment can feel like the end of the world. They might react with a level of frustration that seems over the top, but it's just how they process the emotional whirlwind inside.

Atypical Expressions of Feelings

Now, here's where it gets interesting. The way these emotions come out? Yeah, it's often not what you'd expect. Picture this: a person might face a disappointment and instead of crying or shouting, they just go quiet. It's like watching a movie where the main character suddenly stops talking. Friends and family might scratch their heads, thinking, "What's up with them? Are they not even bothered?" But in reality, they could be feeling a storm of emotions—just not expressing them in the usual way.

This disconnect can lead to some serious misunderstandings. People might assume the individual is indifferent, when in fact, they're grappling with feelings that are just too complex or intense to share in the moment. It's like trying to explain a dream that made perfect sense while you were asleep, but now feels like a jumbled mess.

The Struggle to Articulate Emotions

Let's get real for a second: explaining emotions can be a Herculean task for those with autism. The whole thing relies on a shared understanding of social cues and verbal language—two things that can be pretty tricky for someone on the spectrum. They might feel a wave of happiness or sadness but struggle to find the right words to explain why. It's like having a great story to tell but forgetting the punchline.

This communication gap? It can be frustrating. Picture someone trying to describe a beautiful sunset but only being able to say, "It's nice." That's how it feels for many. They know they're feeling something, but articulating it? That's another story. This often leads to feelings of isolation, as they feel like they're stuck on one side of a glass wall, watching everyone else connect emotionally while they remain on the outside looking in.

Bridging the Emotional Gap

So, how do we bridge this emotional gap? It starts with recognizing and managing emotions effectively. Developing emotional awareness is key. One useful tool? Emotion charts. These bad boys often feature a range of emotions with corresponding facial expressions, helping individuals identify what they're feeling visually. It's like having a cheat sheet for emotions. By pointing to or selecting an emotion that resonates with them, they can kickstart a conversation about their feelings.

And let's not forget about mindfulness. Techniques like deep breathing, meditation, or grounding exercises can be game-changers. These practices help individuals tune into their emotional states without getting overwhelmed. For instance, when anxiety strikes, taking a few deep breaths can create a little bubble of calm, giving them space to reflect on their feelings before reacting. It's like hitting the pause button on a chaotic scene in a movie.

Using Technology and Visual Aids

Another nifty strategy? Using visual aids or technology to express emotions. Some folks find it easier to write down their feelings or use apps designed for emotional expression. These methods provide a safe outlet, allowing individuals to communicate without the pressure of verbalizing their thoughts. In classrooms, teachers can incorporate these tools to help students express themselves during discussions or activities.

Imagine a classroom where a student can pull out an app that helps them articulate how they feel about a group project. Instead of struggling to find the right words, they can simply select from a list of emotions and explain their thoughts. This not only helps the student but also enriches the group's understanding of one another.

Creating a Supportive Environment

Now, let's talk about the importance of creating a supportive environment. Friends, family, and educators play a crucial role in this process. An atmosphere of understanding and patience can make all the difference. Encouraging open dialogue about emotions—even when words are hard to find—can help individuals feel more comfortable sharing what's going on inside.

Instead of asking vague questions like, "How do you feel?" try something more specific, like, "Are you feeling happy or sad right now?" This kind of directness can help guide individuals toward articulating their emotions more clearly. It's like giving them a roadmap to navigate the often murky waters of their feelings.

The Journey of Emotional Recognition

As individuals learn to recognize and manage their emotions, things often start to feel less daunting. With practice, they can develop a vocabulary for their feelings, enabling them to communicate more effectively with others. It's like unlocking a new level in a video game—suddenly, they have the tools to connect with those around them. This newfound ability can lead to stronger relationships and a greater sense of belonging.

Picture a young adult with autism who, after working on emotional awareness, can now express when they're feeling anxious or excited. They're no longer just reacting; they're engaging in conversations about their feelings. This shift can be life-changing, not just for them but for everyone in their orbit.

A Journey of Challenges and Opportunities

Understanding emotions in autism is a journey filled with both challenges and opportunities. By recognizing the unique ways emotions are felt and expressed, we can create a more inclusive and empathetic world. It's not just about helping individuals with autism; it's about enriching the lives of everyone around them.

Encouraging individuals on the spectrum to explore their emotional landscapes while providing them with the tools to articulate their feelings empowers them to connect more deeply with others. It's like planting seeds of understanding that can grow into a beautiful garden of relationships.

Final Thoughts

At the end of the day, fostering emotional awareness benefits everyone. It creates a tapestry of understanding and acceptance, weaving together the diverse experiences of individuals with autism and their neurotypical peers. So, let's champion emotional awareness, support one another, and create a world where everyone can express their feelings freely. After all, we're all in this together, navigating the ups and downs of life, one emotion at a time.

Chapter 8

The Power of Interests and Passions in Autism

When it comes to autism and Asperger's Syndrome, interests and passions aren't just pastimes; they're lifelines. They can spark joy, build confidence, and even create connections with others. So, let's dive into why these deep interests matter and how they shape the lives of those on the spectrum.

A Gateway to Knowledge

You ever notice how some folks can get totally lost in a subject? Like, they can talk about it for hours and never get bored? For many individuals with autism, this isn't just a quirk; it's a powerful learning tool. Picture this: a kid obsessed with dinosaurs. While most kids might just know the T-Rex, this kid's probably memorized every species, their habitats, and extinction theories. That intense focus? It's called *hyperfocus*, and it allows them to dive deep into their passion.

They'll spend hours—no, days—researching, reading, and practicing skills related to their interests. It's like they've got a superpower. They might even become experts, sharing their knowledge with anyone who'll listen. And let's be real—who wouldn't want to know everything about their favorite topic?

Building Confidence

Now, let's talk about confidence. When someone with autism masters a subject, it's a game-changer. That feeling of achievement? It's like winning a gold medal. Suddenly, they feel like they can tackle anything. A kid who knows marine biology inside and out might find it easier to chat with peers, using their passion as a conversation starter. It's a great way to break the ice, turning what could be a nerve-wracking social situation into a chance to connect.

But here's the catch: sometimes, this enthusiasm can lead to misunderstandings. Neurotypical folks might want to chat about the weather or the latest trends, but someone with autism might just keep talking about their favorite dinosaur. It's not that they're trying to hog the spotlight; they're just genuinely excited about what they love.

Finding Balance in Conversations

Navigating social cues can be tricky. It's like walking a tightrope. Friends, family, and teachers need to understand this dynamic. Encouraging individuals to share their passions while also learning to read the room can make a world of difference. Imagine a kid who's passionate about trains. They might start talking about train schedules, and if their friend isn't as into it, they might feel awkward. But if they can find common ground, like discussing favorite train models, that's where the magic happens.

Creating Connections Through Shared Interests

Speaking of common ground, using these passions to connect with others can be a goldmine. When individuals with autism engage in conversations about their interests, they often find others who share that enthusiasm. Picture this: two kids in school, both obsessed with trains. They bond over their favorite models, swap stories, and even play train-themed games. It's a natural way to socialize, allowing them to practice their communication skills without the pressure of typical small talk.

And it's not just a childhood thing. As adults, those passions can be game-changers in the workplace. Employers are increasingly recognizing the unique skills and perspectives that individuals on the spectrum bring to the table. A person with a keen interest in technology? They might shine in roles that require analytical thinking. Their ability to focus on details can lead to innovative solutions that others might miss.

Harnessing Interests in Education

In schools, teachers can tap into these interests to enhance learning experiences. Imagine a teacher designing a project around a student's fascination with space. Instead of a boring textbook lesson, they get to explore scientific concepts through something they love. This not only makes learning fun but empowers students to take charge of their education. It's all about making connections and creating engaging lessons that resonate.

But let's not forget: the autism spectrum is vast. Not every individual will have the same level of interest in specific topics. Some might be all-in on one thing, while others have a wider range of passions. Recognizing this diversity is crucial for providing the right support and encouragement.

Unexpected Opportunities from Passions

Encouraging individuals to explore their interests can lead to some surprising opportunities. Many successful folks on the spectrum have turned their passions into careers or entrepreneurial ventures. Take graphic design, for example. A person who loves it might start their own business, creating logos and branding for clients. Not only does this give them a fulfilling career, but it also connects them with others who appreciate their work.

And in today's digital world, sharing passions has never been easier. Social media and online communities provide platforms for individuals to connect with like-minded people. They can share their knowledge, receive support, and express themselves in ways that feel authentic. It's empowering, really.

The Community Impact of Embracing Passions

In the end, deep interests and passions are vital for individuals with autism and Asperger's Syndrome. They're not just about personal growth; they enhance community understanding. When families, educators, and employers recognize the significance of these interests, they create environments that celebrate the unique talents of those on the spectrum.

Think about it: embracing these passions enriches the lives of individuals with autism while also weaving a richer tapestry in our communities. It fosters understanding and acceptance of neurodiversity, which is something we could all use a bit more of.

So, let's keep the conversation going. Let's celebrate those deep interests, encourage exploration, and support individuals in their passions. After all, when we lift each other up, we all rise together.

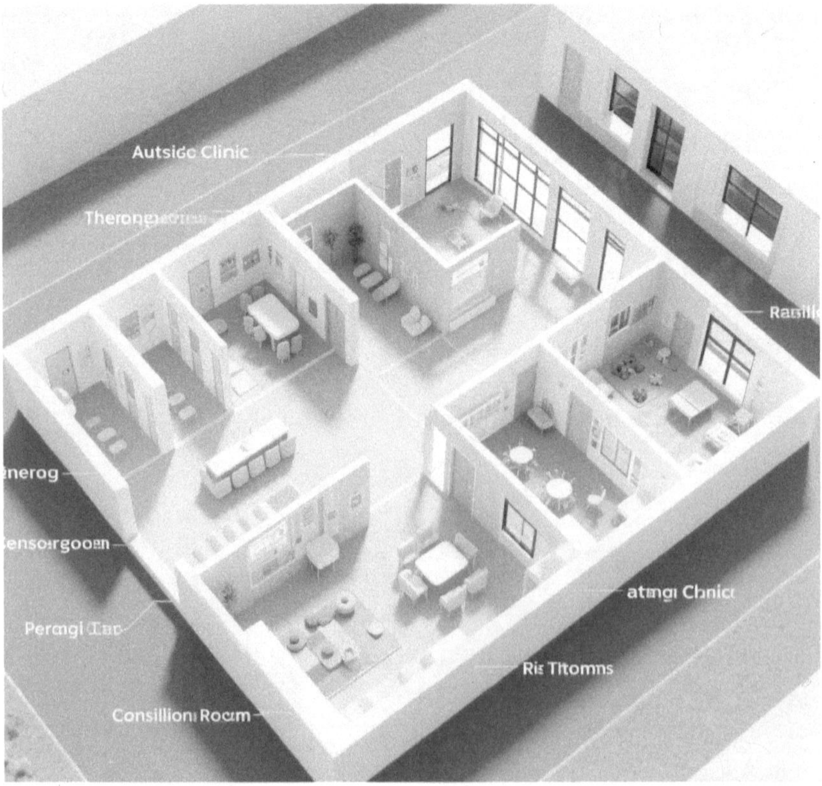

Chapter 9

The Importance of Support Networks

Alright, let's dive into a topic that's near and dear to many hearts: support networks for folks with autism and Asperger's syndrome. You know, when you think about it, having a solid support system is like having a safety net. It's essential for navigating life's ups and downs, especially when you're on the spectrum. Family, friends, and professionals all play pivotal roles in this journey. They're the unsung heroes, really, helping to pave the way for growth, understanding, and acceptance.

Family: The First Line of Defense

Family is usually the first stop on this support train. They know you inside and out—your quirks, your strengths, and yeah, even your weaknesses. Parents, siblings, and even the extended fam can be your biggest cheerleaders. They provide emotional support and create that warm, fuzzy feeling of belonging. Think about it: when you feel secure at home, you're more likely to grow and thrive.

Take a parent, for example. If they get what their kid needs, they can advocate for things like educational accommodations. This means the kid gets the right resources to flourish. Imagine a child who struggles in a traditional classroom but shines in a more tailored learning environment. That's the power of a family that understands.

Friends: The Social Glue

Then you've got friends, who are like the icing on the cake. They can really help boost social skills and create a sense of community. When friends are patient and understanding, they make those overwhelming social situations a bit easier to handle. You know that feeling when you're with someone who just gets you? That's what a supportive friend does. They provide a safe space for you to express yourself, share interests, and practice social skills.

Think about how a good friend can make a world of difference. They help ease feelings of isolation that many individuals with autism face. Just having someone to hang out with can be a game-changer. It's like having a buddy who's got your back, ready to tackle whatever comes your way.

Professionals: The Specialists

Now, let's talk about the pros—teachers, therapists, counselors—you name it. These folks bring specialized knowledge to the table. They offer targeted interventions to tackle specific challenges that come with autism. For instance, a speech therapist can work wonders on communication skills, while an occupational therapist can help with sensory processing issues. It's all about finding the right fit for each individual.

And let's not forget educators. Teachers trained in special

education can create individualized learning plans that cater to a student's unique needs. This tailored approach promotes academic success and personal growth. It's like having a roadmap that guides you through the maze of education.

The Power of Understanding and Patience

Here's the kicker: understanding and patience are the secret sauce in these support networks. When family, friends, and professionals come at it with empathy and an open mind, they create an environment where individuals with autism feel valued. This understanding can manifest in various ways—like recognizing when someone needs a sensory break or acknowledging the hurdles of social communication.

But patience? That's equally crucial. Progress isn't always a straight line. Sometimes it's more like a rollercoaster ride. Individuals with autism might not respond to support in the ways you expect. A patient approach allows them to express themselves at their own pace. Picture a teacher who gets that a student needs a little extra time to process info. That flexibility makes all the difference, building trust and making interactions feel safe.

Real-World Strategies in Schools and Communities

In schools and communities, there are tons of effective support strategies that can really enhance the experiences of individuals with autism. For starters, schools can roll out programs that promote inclusion and understanding among all students. Ever heard of peer mentoring? It's where students with autism get paired up with typically developing peers. This setup not only provides social support for the student with autism but also educates the mentor about neurodiversity. Talk about a win-win!

Community organizations can step up too. Many offer recreational programs specifically designed for individuals on the spectrum. These programs create opportunities for social interaction in a structured environment. Think art classes, sports teams, or social clubs. These activities help individuals build friendships and develop new skills, enhancing their sense of belonging.

Workshops and Training: Spreading the Knowledge

Another effective strategy is hosting workshops and training sessions for family members, educators, and peers. These sessions can provide valuable insights into autism, equipping those in the support network with the tools they need. By fostering a shared understanding of autism, these workshops can help reduce stigma and promote a culture of acceptance. It's all about creating a community that gets it.

Online Communities: A Digital Lifeline

Support networks don't just stop at family and friends. There's a whole world of online communities and support groups out there. These platforms allow individuals and families to share experiences, seek advice, and find encouragement from others facing similar challenges. The anonymity of online forums can be a relief for those who might feel uncomfortable discussing their experiences face-to-face. It's like finding your tribe, even if it's in the digital realm.

The Ripple Effect of Support Networks

So, why does all this matter? Well, the importance of support networks for individuals with autism and Asperger's syndrome is massive. Family, friends, and professionals each play a crucial role in creating a nurturing environment that fosters success and personal growth. Understanding and patience are key components that enhance these relationships, allowing individuals to thrive.

Think about it: when you've got a solid support system, you can tackle life's challenges with a bit more confidence. It's like having a safety net that catches you when you fall. And when schools and communities implement effective support strategies, we move toward a more inclusive society that recognizes and values the unique contributions of individuals with autism.

The Ongoing Journey

Let's not kid ourselves—this journey toward acceptance and understanding is ongoing. But with strong support networks in place, individuals with autism can navigate their paths with confidence and resilience. It's not just about surviving; it's about thriving. And that's what we all want, right?

So, whether you're a family member, a friend, or a professional, remember the impact you can have. You're not just a bystander; you're a vital part of someone's journey. By being there, showing understanding, and practicing patience, you help create a world where individuals with autism can shine.

Final Thoughts

At the end of the day, support networks are like the glue that holds everything together. They provide a sense of belonging, foster growth, and promote understanding. Whether it's family, friends, or professionals, each group has a unique role to play. So, let's celebrate these connections and work together to create a more inclusive world. Because when we support one another, we all win.

Chapter 10

Autism in Different Cultures

Autism is a complex neurodevelopmental condition that manifests in various ways across different cultures. The understanding and treatment of autism vary significantly around the globe, influenced by cultural beliefs, societal norms, and available resources. In some cultures, autism is recognized as a medical condition requiring intervention, while in others, it may be viewed through a spiritual or moral lens. This chapter explores how autism is perceived and treated worldwide, the impact of cultural beliefs on diagnosis and support, and the diverse experiences that broaden our understanding of this condition.

In Western countries, autism is often categorized as a developmental disorder that necessitates medical diagnosis and intervention. The American Psychiatric Association's Diagnostic and Statistical Manual of Mental Disorders (DSM-5) provides specific criteria for diagnosing autism spectrum disorder (ASD). These criteria emphasize observable behaviors and developmental milestones, leading to structured assessment protocols. Consequently, many families in these regions seek early intervention services, such as speech therapy, occupational therapy, and behavioral interventions. The focus is typically on managing symptoms and enhancing the individual's ability to function within society.

Conversely, in many non-Western cultures, autism may not be recognized as a distinct medical condition. In some cases, it is viewed as a manifestation of spiritual issues or a result of familial karma. For instance, in certain Indigenous communities, behaviors associated with autism might be interpreted as signs of a spiritual gift or a connection to the spirit world. Such beliefs can lead to alternative forms of support, including community rituals, traditional healing practices, or guidance from elders. In these contexts, the emphasis is often on acceptance and integration within the community rather than on clinical intervention.

Cultural beliefs significantly affect the diagnosis and support systems available to individuals with autism. In societies where mental health awareness is limited, families may face stigma or misunderstanding. Parents might be reluctant to seek help due to fears of social ostracism or shame. For example, in some Asian cultures, the concept of "saving face" can prevent families from acknowledging a diagnosis of autism, leading to isolation and a lack of resources. The result is often a cycle of misunderstanding and inadequate support for individuals on the spectrum.

In contrast, cultures that prioritize collectivism may offer a different approach to support. In these societies, the extended family plays a crucial role in the upbringing of children, including those with autism. This support network can provide emotional and practical assistance, helping families navigate challenges together. For instance, in many African cultures, community-based initiatives may offer resources and support for families affected by autism, promoting inclusion and understanding within the community.

Stories of diverse experiences provide valuable insights into how autism is perceived and treated across cultures. In Japan, for example, the concept of "hikikomori" refers to individuals who withdraw from social life, often linked to autism and other mental health conditions. While this phenomenon is frequently viewed negatively, some individuals and families embrace it as a legitimate lifestyle choice, reflecting cultural values around privacy and personal space. This perspective challenges the notion that social engagement is universally desirable and highlights the importance of understanding individual preferences.

In contrast, the experience of autism in Scandinavian countries often emphasizes inclusivity and support. These nations have made significant strides in creating environments that accommodate individuals with autism. For instance, Denmark offers specialized education programs that focus on the strengths of students with autism, fostering their unique abilities while providing necessary support. The emphasis on acceptance and integration in these cultures reflects a broader societal commitment to neurodiversity, encouraging individuals to thrive within their communities.

The narratives of individuals with autism also shed light on the varied experiences shaped by cultural contexts. A young woman from Brazil, diagnosed with autism, shares her journey of self-acceptance and empowerment. Despite facing challenges in her community, she found solace in art, using her creativity to express her thoughts and emotions. Her story illustrates how personal interests can serve as a bridge to connect with others, transcending cultural barriers and fostering understanding.

Similarly, a young man from Nigeria recounts his experience navigating life with autism in a society where awareness is limited. He describes the support he received from his family and friends, who embraced his unique qualities. Through their encouragement, he developed a passion for technology, eventually pursuing a career in software development. His story highlights the potential for individuals with autism to excel when provided with the right support and opportunities.

These diverse experiences underscore the importance of recognizing the cultural dimensions of autism. By understanding how autism is viewed and treated in different societies, we can foster a more inclusive dialogue that respects individual experiences and cultural contexts. This approach encourages us to challenge preconceived notions about autism and consider the myriad ways in which individuals can thrive, regardless of their cultural background.

As we continue to explore autism through a global lens, it becomes clear that there is no one-size-fits-all approach to diagnosis and support. Instead, we must embrace the complexity of autism as it intersects with culture, recognizing that each individual's experience is shaped by a unique combination of factors. By valuing diverse perspectives, we can create a more nuanced understanding of autism that transcends borders and fosters acceptance.

In conclusion, the exploration of autism in different cultures reveals a rich tapestry of beliefs, practices, and experiences. From the medicalized views prevalent in Western societies to the spiritual interpretations found in many Indigenous cultures, the ways in which autism is understood and treated are profoundly influenced by cultural context. As we broaden our understanding of autism, we must remain open to the diverse narratives that challenge our assumptions and enrich our perspectives. By fostering inclusivity and embracing neurodiversity, we can create a world where individuals with autism are valued for their unique contributions and supported in their journeys toward fulfillment and success.

Chapter 11

The Journey of Diagnosis

The journey to an autism diagnosis can be a complex and emotional experience for families and individuals. Understanding what happens during an autism assessment, the significance of early diagnosis, and the feelings that accompany this process is crucial for navigating this path.

An autism assessment typically begins with a comprehensive evaluation. Parents or caregivers often initiate the process by expressing concerns about a child's development. This may include difficulties with communication, social interactions, or behavioral patterns that seem atypical. The first step is usually a visit to a pediatrician or a psychologist specializing in developmental disorders. During this initial consultation, healthcare professionals gather information about the child's medical history, developmental milestones, and any observed behaviors that raise concern.

Following this initial meeting, a series of assessments are conducted. These assessments can vary but generally include standardized tests that measure communication skills, social behavior, and cognitive abilities. Clinicians may observe the child in various settings, such as at home or in school, to get a fuller picture of their behavior. Parent interviews and questionnaires are also vital components of the assessment process. These tools help professionals understand the child's strengths and challenges, providing a more nuanced view of their development.

The assessment process can take time, often spanning several weeks or even months. This duration can be a source of anxiety for families. Parents may feel a mix of hope and fear as they await results. Will their child receive a diagnosis? What will that mean for their future? The uncertainty can be overwhelming, but it is essential to remember that a thorough assessment is crucial for an accurate diagnosis.

Early diagnosis of autism can significantly alter the trajectory of a child's life. Research indicates that identifying autism at a young age allows for timely interventions that can greatly improve developmental outcomes. Early intervention programs, which may include speech therapy, occupational therapy, or behavioral therapies, can help children develop essential skills. These programs are designed to support communication, social skills, and daily living skills, providing children with the tools they need to navigate their environments more effectively.

When children receive early intervention, they often show remarkable progress. Skills that may take longer to develop without support can flourish with the right resources. For instance, a child who struggles with communication may learn to express their needs more effectively, reducing frustration for both the child and their family. Similarly, social skills training can help children understand social cues and engage more comfortably with peers, fostering friendships and a sense of belonging.

The emotional landscape for families during this journey is

multifaceted. Parents often experience a whirlwind of feelings, from anxiety and confusion to relief and determination. Many parents report feeling a sense of isolation as they navigate the complexities of the assessment process. They may worry about their child's future and grapple with societal misconceptions about autism. The fear of stigma can be palpable, leading some families to delay seeking an assessment or to feel uncertain about how to advocate for their child.

As families engage with professionals, they may also encounter a sense of hope. The prospect of receiving a diagnosis can bring clarity. Understanding that their child's challenges have a name can be empowering. It allows parents to seek out resources, connect with support networks, and advocate for their child's needs more effectively. The journey of diagnosis can be a catalyst for families to learn more about autism, fostering a greater understanding of their child's unique strengths and challenges.

However, the emotional journey does not end with a diagnosis. Many families report feeling a mix of relief and sadness upon receiving the news. Relief comes from finally having answers and a path forward. Sadness may arise from the realization that their child will face unique challenges in a world that can be unaccommodating. This duality of emotions is natural and underscores the complexity of the experience.

Families often find themselves reflecting on their child's journey up to this point. They may revisit milestones, considering whether certain behaviors were indicative of autism. This introspection can lead to a deeper understanding of their child’s needs and strengths. It also opens the door to conversations about acceptance and advocacy, as families learn to embrace their child's neurodiversity.

As individuals undergo the assessment process, their feelings can vary widely. Some may feel anxious about being evaluated, while others might experience a sense of relief in finally being heard. For older children and adults, the process can evoke feelings of vulnerability. They may worry about how a diagnosis will impact their relationships, education, or career prospects. The journey of diagnosis is not just about receiving a label; it is about understanding oneself in a new light.

Navigating the assessment process requires patience and resilience. Families must often advocate for their child, pushing for assessments and interventions that meet their unique needs. This advocacy can be daunting, especially in a system that may not always prioritize individual differences. However, many families find strength in community. Support groups, both online and in-person, provide a space for sharing experiences, resources, and encouragement.

Ultimately, the journey of diagnosis is a pivotal moment in the lives of individuals with autism and their families. It is a process that, while challenging, can lead to greater understanding and support. The importance of early diagnosis cannot be overstated; it opens doors to interventions that can significantly enhance a child's development. As families navigate this journey, they learn to embrace their child's uniqueness, fostering an environment of acceptance and growth.

In conclusion, the assessment process is more than just a series of tests; it is a journey filled with emotions, reflections, and newfound understanding. Families and individuals alike emerge from this process with a deeper appreciation for the complexities of autism. As they move forward, they carry with them the knowledge that their journey is just beginning—a journey of advocacy, acceptance, and celebration of neurodiversity.

Chapter 12

Autism and Education: Navigating Unique Learning Needs

Getting a grip on how to educate students with autism means diving into their one-of-a-kind learning styles. Each kid on the autism spectrum comes with their own set of challenges and strengths, which can totally change their school experience. These differences often arise from how they process sensory information, communicate, and think. For instance, some might shine with visual learning, while others might be all about auditory or hands-on methods. Spotting these varied learning styles is key for teachers who want to build an inclusive classroom that encourages growth and keeps kids engaged.

The Autism Experience in the Classroom

Kids with autism often have a different way of processing info compared to their neurotypical classmates. They might be super sensitive to sensory input, which can make it tough for them to focus in a typical classroom. Picture this: a child who can't handle loud noises might zone out during a chaotic class discussion where everyone's talking at once. On the flip side, some students might thrive in a space bursting with visual aids —think charts, diagrams, and videos—that help them grasp tricky concepts. By understanding these individual quirks, teachers can tweak their teaching styles to better fit each student's needs.

Personalized Teaching: The Game Changer

Personalized teaching methods are vital for making the learning experience better for students with autism. We're not just talking about sticking to the standard curriculum; it's about reshaping content, teaching strategies, and assessments to match each student's unique learning profile. When teachers personalize their approach, they open doors for students to connect with the material in ways that click with them. This can boost motivation, help them remember stuff better, and lead to greater academic success overall.

Visual Supports: A Simple Yet Effective Tool

One solid method in personalized teaching is using visual supports. Take visual schedules, for example. They lay out daily activities clearly, helping students anticipate changes and ease anxiety. Graphic organizers are another handy tool—they help students structure their thoughts, making it easier for them to organize their work and express what they understand. By weaving visual elements into lessons, teachers can help students with autism better grasp and retain information.

Hands-On Learning: Getting Into the Action

Another important part of personalized teaching is incorporating hands-on learning experiences. Many students with autism thrive when they can physically engage with materials and apply concepts in real-world ways. Imagine a science lesson about ecosystems where students create a small terrarium. They'd get to see how plants and animals interact up close. These experiential learning opportunities don't just make the material relatable; they also build critical thinking and problem-solving skills.

Adapting the Classroom Environment

Successful classroom adaptations can take the educational experience for students with autism to the next level. These changes can range from physical modifications in the classroom to tweaks in teaching practices. For instance, setting up a designated quiet area in the classroom can give students a retreat when they feel overwhelmed. This space could have calming tools like fidget toys or noise-canceling headphones, allowing students to self-regulate and jump back into learning when they're ready.

Flexible Grouping: Building Connections

On top of physical adaptations, teachers can use flexible grouping strategies to encourage collaboration and social interaction among students. Pairing students with autism with neurotypical peers during group activities can facilitate social learning and bridge communication gaps. By nurturing positive peer relationships, educators can cultivate a supportive classroom culture that helps all students thrive.

Tech-Savvy Learning: Embracing the Digital Age

Let's not forget about technology—it can be a game changer for students with autism. There's a whole bunch of educational apps and software designed to cater to different learning styles, offering interactive and engaging ways for students to learn. For example, speech-to-text software can help those who struggle with writing, letting them express their ideas more freely. Educational games focusing on social skills can also provide a low-pressure environment for students to practice essential interpersonal interactions.

Teamwork Makes the Dream Work

Collaboration among educators, parents, and specialists is crucial. Keeping the lines of communication open ensures that students get the support they need to thrive academically and socially. Regular meetings to discuss progress, challenges, and strategies for improvement foster a team approach to education, ultimately benefiting the student. When families are involved, they can share valuable insights about their child's strengths and preferences, helping educators make informed decisions about teaching methods and classroom adjustments.

The Power of Early Intervention

Research backs up the idea that early intervention and personalized education can lead to positive outcomes for students with autism. Tailoring educational experiences to meet individual needs not only boosts academic performance but also promotes social skills and emotional well-being. As more educators embrace personalized teaching methods and classroom adaptations, the chances for students with autism to thrive in educational settings increase significantly.

Creating an Inclusive Environment

In conclusion, grasping the unique learning styles of students with autism is crucial for crafting an effective educational environment. By implementing personalized teaching methods and making thoughtful classroom adaptations, educators can support the diverse needs of these students. As we keep exploring innovative strategies and approaches, the goal remains clear: to provide every student with the opportunity to succeed and flourish in their educational journey. The future of education for students with autism is bright, filled with possibilities for growth, understanding, and acceptance.

Breaking Down Barriers: Real-Life Impacts

Let's take a moment to reflect on what this all means in real life. Imagine a classroom where a child with autism, let's call him Alex, struggles to keep up. Traditional teaching methods don't resonate with him, and he often feels lost in the shuffle. But with personalized teaching strategies in place—like visual schedules and hands-on activities—Alex starts to find his footing. He creates a terrarium for his science project, and suddenly, he's engaged. He's asking questions, making observations, and even collaborating with classmates.

This isn't just a win for Alex; it's a win for everyone in the classroom. His peers learn empathy and teamwork, and teachers gain valuable insights into how to reach diverse learners.

The Bigger Picture: Society's Role

Now, let's zoom out a bit. Education isn't just about individual students; it's about shaping society. When we invest in personalized education for students with autism, we're not just helping them succeed in school. We're setting the stage for them to thrive in life. These students grow up to be adults who contribute to their communities, bringing unique perspectives and skills to the table.

It's a win-win. Society benefits when we embrace diversity and inclusion. When we give students with autism the tools they need to succeed, we're paving the way for a more understanding and accepting world.

A Call to Action

So, what can we do to support this movement? First off, let's advocate for more resources in schools—more training for teachers, more tools for personalized learning, and more collaboration between families and educators. It's about creating a culture that values every learner, no matter their background or challenges.

We can also raise awareness in our communities. Talk to friends, family, and neighbors about the importance of inclusive education. Share stories of success, like Alex's, to inspire others to get involved.

Final Thoughts: The Road Ahead

As we navigate this journey, let's remember that the road to understanding and acceptance is ongoing. It takes effort, patience, and a willingness to learn. But every step we take towards creating an inclusive educational environment is a step towards a brighter future for students with autism.

Let's keep pushing boundaries, challenging norms, and

advocating for change. Together, we can create classrooms where every student feels valued, understood, and ready to take on the world.

The future isn't just bright for students with autism—it's downright dazzling. And it's up to us to make sure they have every opportunity to shine.

Chapter 13

Employment and Autism: Bridging the Gap

When you think about work, what comes to mind? A paycheck? Sure. But for many adults with autism, it's about so much more than just making ends meet. It's about finding purpose, feeling like they belong, and showcasing their unique skills. For those on the autism spectrum, meaningful employment isn't just a job; it's a crucial part of their identity and self-worth. But let's be real—getting there isn't always a walk in the park.

The road to employment for adults with autism is often riddled with bumps. There's a ton of misunderstanding out there about what autism really is, and that lack of awareness can create some serious barriers. It's like trying to climb a mountain with a backpack full of rocks. Misconceptions about their capabilities can lead employers to overlook talented individuals who could bring fresh perspectives and skills to their teams.

Why Meaningful Work Matters

So, why do adults with autism crave meaningful work? It boils down to a few key motivations. First off, there's this strong desire to contribute to society. They want to be part of something bigger than themselves—a team, a project, a mission. Many of them are driven by their interests and strengths. Think about it: people on the spectrum often have incredible attention to detail, sharp analytical skills, and the ability to dive deep into specific tasks. These aren't just traits; they're superpowers!

Yet, despite these strengths, a lot of employers don't realize the goldmine of talent they're missing out on. They might not know how to tap into the unique skills that neurodiverse individuals can bring to the table. It's like having a treasure chest full of gems but not knowing how to open it.

Making Workplaces More Inclusive

But here's the kicker: workplaces can be tweaked to better support employees with autism. By making reasonable adjustments, companies can create a more inclusive and productive environment. For example, how about designing a sensory-friendly workspace? This could mean lowering noise levels, providing noise-canceling headphones, or even allowing employees to choose their lighting. Small changes can make a world of difference.

And let's not forget about communication. Clear, straightforward instructions can help individuals with autism navigate their roles more effectively. Employers can also promote an inclusive culture by offering training sessions on autism and neurodiversity. When staff understands what autism is and how to support their colleagues, it fosters a sense of belonging and acceptance.

Real-Life Success Stories

Now, let's dive into some success stories that really highlight how meaningful employment can change lives. Take a young guy who dreamed of becoming a software developer. He hit a wall when it came to job interviews—those preconceived notions about autism made it tough for him to get his foot in the door. But then, he found a mentor who believed in him and an employer who was willing to think outside the box. Instead of the usual interview process, they let him showcase his skills through practical assessments. This not only proved his technical abilities but also allowed him to shine in problem-solving. Fast forward to today, and he's thriving in a role that plays to his strengths and gives him a sense of community.

Or consider a talented graphic designer who had a passion for visual arts. She faced a tough job market, with many employers overlooking her amazing portfolio because of her communication challenges. But then, a forward-thinking company saw her potential and offered her a position that allowed her to work independently while still collaborating with a small team. This setup helped her unleash her creativity, leading to successful projects and a career she loves.

These stories are just a couple of examples, but they underscore a crucial point: recognizing the strengths of individuals with autism is key. When employers take the time to understand what neurodiverse individuals can offer, they not only create a more inclusive workplace but also unlock a treasure trove of talent that can drive innovation and success.

Shifting the Narrative

As society's understanding of autism evolves, it's time for the narrative around employment to shift too. We need to embrace neurodiversity and advocate for meaningful work opportunities. Imagine a future where individuals with autism aren't just employed but are celebrated for their contributions. That transformation starts with awareness and understanding, leading to real changes in the workplace that benefit everyone.

Let's face it: the intersection of autism and employment is complex, but it's also filled with promise. Adults with autism want work that aligns with their strengths and interests. By making necessary adjustments in the workplace and sharing inspiring success stories, we can create an environment that supports neurodiverse individuals. It's not just about accommodating differences; it's about recognizing the immense value that diversity brings to our professional lives.

The Bigger Picture

Now, let's zoom out for a second. The conversation around autism and employment isn't just about individuals; it's about the larger society. When we create inclusive workplaces, we're not just helping a few people; we're enriching our communities and economies. Diverse teams lead to better problem-solving, creativity, and innovation. It's a win-win!

Think about it: when neurodiverse individuals are given the opportunity to thrive, they can contribute in ways that others might not even consider. Their unique perspectives can lead to breakthroughs in technology, art, science, and beyond. Plus, fostering an inclusive environment can improve morale and job satisfaction for everyone on the team. Who wouldn't want to work in a place where everyone feels valued and respected?

The Role of Employers

Employers have a critical role to play in this shift. They need to be proactive about creating an inclusive culture. This means not just hiring individuals with autism but also providing ongoing support and resources. Regular check-ins, mentorship programs, and opportunities for professional development can make a huge difference. It's about building a foundation where everyone feels empowered to succeed.

And let's not forget about collaboration. Employers should work with organizations that specialize in supporting individuals with autism. These partnerships can help bridge the gap between job seekers and employers, ensuring that everyone has the tools they need to succeed.

Advocacy and Awareness

On the flip side, advocacy is crucial. We need to spread the word about the capabilities of individuals with autism. Awareness campaigns can help dispel myths and misconceptions, making it easier for employers to see the potential in neurodiverse candidates. Sharing success stories, like those mentioned earlier, can inspire change and encourage others to take action.

And hey, let's not underestimate the power of community. When individuals with autism come together, they can share experiences, support each other, and advocate for their rights. Community organizations can provide valuable resources, networking opportunities, and mentorship programs that can make a real difference in job seekers' lives.

A Call to Action

So, what can you do? Whether you're an employer, an employee, or just someone who cares, there are steps you can take to make a difference. If you're in a position of power, consider how you can make your workplace more inclusive. If you're an employee, advocate for your colleagues and help raise awareness. And if you're just someone who wants to help, educate yourself and others about autism and neurodiversity.

Together, we can create a future where individuals with autism are not just accepted but celebrated for their unique contributions. It's about building a society that values diversity and recognizes the strengths of every individual.

In Conclusion

The journey to meaningful employment for adults with autism is complex but filled with potential. By understanding their motivations, making necessary adjustments in the workplace, and sharing success stories, we can foster an environment that supports neurodiverse individuals. It's not just about accommodating differences; it's about recognizing the immense value that diversity brings to our professional lives.

As we champion the rights and abilities of individuals with autism, we pave the way for a more inclusive and equitable future for everyone. So, let's roll up our sleeves and get to work—together, we can make a difference!

Chapter 14

The Future of Autism Research: A New Dawn in Understanding

The landscape of autism research is shifting dramatically, thanks to groundbreaking technologies. We're talking about some serious brain science here. New tools are helping us peel back the layers of the brain, especially when it comes to understanding autism and Asperger's Syndrome. The days of guessing are over; now we can actually see what's going on in there.

Visualizing the Brain: A Game Changer

Ever heard of functional magnetic resonance imaging (fMRI) or positron emission tomography (PET) scans? These are the rock stars of brain imaging. They let researchers watch how different parts of the brain light up during various tasks. It's like having a front-row seat to a concert where the brain is the star performer.

What's fascinating is how these technologies reveal the unique ways people on the autism spectrum process information. For example, fMRI studies show that while neurotypical folks activate certain brain areas when looking at faces, individuals with autism might engage entirely different neural pathways. This isn't just academic mumbo jumbo; it's a treasure trove of insights that can lead to tailored interventions. By figuring out these distinct brain patterns, researchers can craft strategies that cater specifically to the needs of those on the spectrum.

Genetics Meets Environment: The Big Picture

But wait, there's more! Genetic research is digging deep into the autism puzzle, and it's not just about genes. Sure, twin and family studies highlight the genetic predisposition to autism, but the environment is also a player in this game. Factors like prenatal exposure to medications, maternal infections, and even pollution are now recognized as key contributors.

Understanding how these elements interact is crucial for crafting effective prevention strategies. It's like a dance between genetics and the environment, and we're just starting to learn the steps. Researchers are now diving into epigenetics, which looks at how environmental factors can tweak gene expression without changing the DNA itself. This field is opening up new doors for understanding how things like diet and lifestyle can influence autism risk. Imagine if we could pinpoint specific environmental triggers; we could potentially reduce the chances of autism developing in the first place.

Innovative Treatments on the Horizon

As we dig deeper into the biological roots of autism, the future of treatment options looks brighter than ever. Traditional interventions often revolve around behavioral therapies, which are super important for building social skills and communication. But here's the kicker: new research is hinting that medications might also help tackle some of the core challenges faced by individuals with autism.

Think about it—medications that target neurotransmitter systems related to mood and anxiety could provide an extra layer of support. It's like having a toolkit that combines both behavioral and pharmacological approaches to address the unique challenges of autism.

Tech Takes the Stage: Personalizing Interventions

And let's not forget about technology. It's making waves in therapeutic practices, paving the way for more personalized and effective interventions. Virtual reality (VR) and augmented reality (AR) are becoming the new kids on the block for teaching social skills. Imagine stepping into a virtual world where you can practice social interactions without the pressure of real-life consequences. That's what VR offers—a safe space to learn and grow.

These immersive experiences provide instant feedback, allowing individuals with autism to adjust their responses in real time. It's like having a personal coach right there with you, guiding you through the complexities of social situations.

Artificial Intelligence: The Brain's New Best Friend

Now, let's talk about artificial intelligence (AI). This isn't just sci-fi stuff; AI is stepping up to the plate in autism research. Machine learning algorithms can sift through mountains of data—behavioral patterns, genetic info, environmental factors—looking for connections that might slip past human researchers.

This capability is a game changer. By identifying patterns, AI can help create predictive models that spot individuals at risk for autism or those who might benefit from specific interventions. It's like having a crystal ball that helps researchers discover new insights and refine existing treatment approaches faster than ever.

Collaboration: The Key to Progress

But here's the real kicker: collaboration. The future of autism research isn't just about one discipline; it's about bringing together neuroscience, genetics, psychology, and technology. Interdisciplinary teams are popping up everywhere, pooling their expertise to tackle the tough challenges associated with autism.

This collaborative spirit enriches the research process and sparks innovation in treatment development. When researchers share their findings across disciplines, it opens up a world of possibilities. The potential for breakthroughs is huge, and as we combine our knowledge, we can create a more comprehensive understanding of autism.

The Road Ahead: A Bright Future

So, what does the future hold for autism research? It's looking pretty darn bright. With rapid advancements in technology and a deeper understanding of the genetic and environmental factors at play, we're on the cusp of unlocking new possibilities for support and treatment.

As we continue to explore the complexities of the brain, we're not just gathering knowledge; we're crafting a roadmap for better interventions. The integration of innovative technologies and interdisciplinary collaboration holds the promise of enhancing the lives of individuals with autism and their families.

Imagine a world where we embrace neurodiversity, recognizing the unique strengths of individuals on the autism spectrum. It's not just about understanding autism; it's about creating a more inclusive society. The journey toward a better understanding of autism is ongoing, but with each discovery, we're getting closer to a future where individuals with autism can truly thrive.

Final Thoughts: Embracing Change

In conclusion, the future of autism research is not just a scientific endeavor; it's a movement. It's about harnessing the power of technology, genetics, and collaboration to create a brighter tomorrow for those on the autism spectrum. As we embrace these developments, we're not just changing the narrative around autism; we're transforming lives.

So, let's keep pushing forward, exploring the unknown, and breaking down barriers. The journey may be long, but every step brings us closer to a world that values neurodiversity and supports individuals with autism in living their best lives. Let's make it happen!

Chapter 15

Celebrating Neurodiversity: Embracing Our Unique Minds

Neurodiversity isn't just a buzzword; it's a powerful movement that shines a light on the incredible variety of human thinking. You see, the brain's wiring isn't one-size-fits-all. It varies, and that variation—like what we see in autism or Asperger's Syndrome—shouldn't be seen as a problem to fix. Nah, it's a treasure trove of unique perspectives that enrich our world. This way of thinking flips the script on neurodevelopmental conditions, shifting the focus from what's "wrong" to what's "right." It's about recognizing the strengths and potential that come with these differences.

Let's get real: being different is crucial for progress. History's full of folks who thought outside the box and, boy, did they change the game. Think about the inventors, artists, and scientists who shook things up. Their offbeat ideas and unconventional approaches led to breakthroughs that we might never have seen if everyone thought the same. And guess what? This applies to those on the autism spectrum, too. Their unique thought processes can spark amazing insights and innovations. If we embrace these differences, we're not just being nice; we're tapping into a wellspring of potential that can benefit society as a whole.

When you throw a bunch of diverse thinkers into the mix,

magic happens. Seriously! Different cognitive styles create a hotbed for creativity and problem-solving. It's like a potluck dinner where everyone brings their best dish—together, they create a feast. In workplaces, teams that include neurodiverse individuals often kick butt compared to more uniform groups. Why? Because they tackle problems from all sorts of angles, leading to solutions that are way more comprehensive. It's not just talk; studies back this up. Companies that embrace diversity—especially neurodiversity—tend to see boosts in innovation and success. It's like having a secret weapon.

So, how do we really make the most of neurodiversity? First off, we gotta promote acceptance and inclusion. This starts with education. Schools and workplaces need to step up and offer training that highlights the value of neurodiversity. Imagine teaching folks about the strengths that come with different cognitive styles. It's all about creating an atmosphere of understanding and respect. Plus, we need practical strategies to accommodate diverse needs, ensuring everyone gets a fair shot at contributing.

Another biggie? Amplifying the voices of neurodiverse individuals. We need to give them platforms to share their stories, insights, and talents. When society hears directly from those who see the world differently, it builds empathy. Storytelling is a powerful tool here. By sharing their personal narratives, people on the autism spectrum can shed light on the unique challenges they face while showcasing their strengths. This isn't just about raising awareness; it's about humanizing their experiences and helping others see the value in diversity.

Community engagement is crucial, too. Local organizations, schools, and businesses should team up to create inclusive events that celebrate neurodiversity. Think art exhibitions featuring neurodiverse artists or community forums discussing the importance of inclusion. Bringing people together fosters a sense of belonging and mutual support—

essential ingredients for acceptance.

And let's not forget about media representation. How films, TV shows, and books portray neurodiverse characters matters a lot. When these characters are depicted authentically, it helps normalize their experiences and challenges. Good representation can smash stereotypes and misconceptions, paving the way for greater understanding. Media creators have a responsibility to show neurodiversity in a nuanced and respectful way, highlighting the full range of experiences and talents.

Advocacy is another piece of the puzzle. Individuals and organizations committed to neurodiversity can work to change policies and public perceptions. This means pushing for legislation that supports neurodiverse individuals in education, employment, and healthcare. By advocating for systemic changes, we can create a society that truly values the contributions of everyone.

Now, here's the kicker: celebrating neurodiversity isn't a one-and-done deal. It's an ongoing journey. It takes continuous effort, education, and a willingness to reflect. Society needs to challenge its biases and assumptions, recognizing that everyone has something valuable to bring to the table. By fostering an environment where differences are celebrated rather than stigmatized, we can unlock the potential of neurodiverse individuals and enrich our communities.

In wrapping this up, let's remember that celebrating neurodiversity is about more than just recognizing differences. It's about understanding their significance and the benefits they bring to society. By embracing diverse ways of thinking, promoting acceptance, and creating inclusive spaces, we can harness the strengths of all individuals. Building a more inclusive society is a team effort that requires commitment and action from everyone. Together, we can create a future where neurodiversity is not just accepted but celebrated as a vital part of our shared humanity.

Why It Matters: The Real-World Impact of Neurodiversity

Alright, let's dig deeper. Why does all this matter? Because embracing neurodiversity isn't just a feel-good idea; it's a game-changer. Picture this: a workplace where everyone feels valued and understood. Employees who know their strengths and are supported in their unique ways can be more productive and engaged. That's not just good for them; it's great for business. Companies that prioritize neurodiversity often see lower turnover rates and higher employee satisfaction. Happy employees? That's a win-win.

But it goes beyond the workplace. Think about how neurodiversity can enhance education. When schools recognize and celebrate different learning styles, they create environments where all students can thrive. Imagine classrooms that cater to various cognitive needs, allowing students to shine in their own ways. This not only boosts academic performance but also fosters self-esteem and confidence. Kids who feel understood are more likely to engage and succeed.

And let's talk about innovation. The world needs fresh ideas, and diverse thinkers are often the ones to deliver them. In fields like tech, healthcare, and the arts, neurodiverse individuals have made significant contributions. Their unique perspectives can lead to breakthroughs that benefit everyone. So, when society embraces neurodiversity, it's not just doing the right thing; it's paving the way for a brighter future.

Personal Anecdote: A Real-Life Example

Let me share a quick story. I once worked with a guy named Jake. He was on the autism spectrum, and at first, people didn't know what to make of him. But once we got to know him, it was clear he had an incredible knack for problem-solving. He saw patterns and connections that others missed. In team meetings, while everyone was brainstorming the usual ideas, Jake would throw out suggestions that were totally outside the box. At first, we were skeptical, but over time, his ideas led to some of our most successful projects.

Jake's experience is a testament to what happens when we embrace neurodiversity. Instead of seeing him as "different" or "challenging," we learned to appreciate his unique contributions. It wasn't just a win for Jake; it was a win for the whole team.

The Future: Building a Neurodiverse Society

Looking ahead, the goal is clear: we need to build a society that fully embraces neurodiversity. This means continuing to advocate for policies that support neurodiverse individuals in all areas of life. It means pushing for inclusive practices in schools, workplaces, and communities.

And let's not forget the role of technology. With the rise of remote work and digital communication, there are more opportunities than ever for neurodiverse individuals to thrive. Companies can leverage technology to create flexible work environments that cater to diverse needs. This isn't just about convenience; it's about creating spaces where everyone can contribute their best work.

Wrapping It Up: A Call to Action

So, what can you do? Start by educating yourself and those around you. Engage in conversations about neurodiversity. Share what you've learned, and challenge misconceptions when you hear them. Support organizations that advocate for neurodiversity and inclusion. Whether it's volunteering your time, donating, or simply spreading the word, every little bit helps.

And if you're in a position of influence—whether in a workplace, school, or community—take action. Push for training on neurodiversity. Advocate for policies that support inclusion. Create spaces where diverse thinkers can thrive.

At the end of the day, celebrating neurodiversity is about recognizing the beauty in our differences. It's about creating a world where everyone feels valued and empowered to share their unique gifts. So let's roll up our sleeves and get to work. Together, we can build a future where neurodiversity isn't just accepted but celebrated as an essential part of who we are.

Chapter 15

NOTES

Profile of Autism in Children:

Autism Spectrum Disorder (ASD) is a neurodevelopmental condition characterized by challenges in social communication and interaction, alongside restricted, repetitive patterns of behaviour, interests, or activities. The spectrum nature means symptoms and severity vary widely among individuals.

Typical signs in children may include:

Difficulty with verbal and non-verbal communication

Challenges in understanding social cues and forming relationships

Repetitive behaviours (e.g., hand-flapping, rocking)

Strong preference for routines and resistance to change

Sensory sensitivities (over- or under-reactivity to sounds, textures, lights)

Common Methods of Treatment:

1. **Early Intervention:** Early diagnosis and intervention can significantly improve outc Programs often begin in toddler years.
2. **Behavioural Therapies:**
    - **Applied Behaviour Analysis (ABA):** Focuses on reinforcing positive beha and reducing harmful or disruptive ones.
    - **Developmental, Individual differences, Relationship-based (DIR/Floor-time):** Emphasizes emotional and relational development.
3. **Speech and Language Therapy:** Helps improve communication skills, both verb non-verbal.
4. **Occupational Therapy:** Aims to enhance daily living skills and sensory integration.

5. **Social Skills Training:** Teaches children how to interact more effectively with peers.
6. **Medication:** No cure exists, but medications may help manage symptoms like anxiety, hyperactivity, or irritability when necessary.
7. **Family Support and Education:** Empowering families with knowledge and coping strategies is vital.

Treatment plans are highly individualized, depending on the child's unique strengths and challenges. Multidisciplinary approaches often yield the best results.

www.ingramcontent.com/pod-product-compliance
Lightning Source LLC
LaVergne TN
LVHW101616210926
848480LV00009B/679